INSIDE COMMUNISM

Douglas Hyde

Comprising

COMMUNISM FROM THE INSIDE
1948

COMMUNISM AND THE HOME
1950

CATHOLIC TRUTH SOCIETY
PUBLISHERS TO THE HOLY SEE

There is nothing to be gained
from dishonest anti-Communist
propaganda... Let our weapons
in the fight against it be truth,
understanding and Christian action.

Once a Methodist lay preacher and active Communist,
Douglas Hyde (1911-1996) became a Catholic in 1948.

CTS ONEFIFTIES

Originally published as *Communism from the Inside*, 1948;
Communism and the Home, 1950.

Published by The Incorporated Catholic Truth Society,
40-46 Harleyford Road, London SE11 5AY

www.ctsbooks.org

All rights reserved.

Copyright © 2017 The Incorporated Catholic Truth Society.

ISBN 978 1 78469 540 8

COMMUNISM FROM THE INSIDE

Douglas Hyde

A PERSONAL NOTE

This pamphlet is written on the basis of my own personal experience. For twenty years, from the time I was seventeen, I was a member of the Communist Party, holding positions at all levels of the organization. I held responsible positions in a large number of its 'satellite' bodies, spoke for it, wrote for it, lived for it.

For eight years I was employed as an executive on the Communist paper, *The Daily Worker*, as chief sub-editor, then chief reporter, and finally for five years as news editor.

My reasons for resigning and seeking to become a Catholic have been told elsewhere. But it should be understood that I, too, believed, preached, and spread the ideas which are here explained and exposed. I know from experience the hold which they can have on men's minds, the effect they have on men's lives, and their power for untold evil.

And, having found the only possible alternative to Communism in the Catholic Church, I know the need for combating Communism and all its works. It is my hope that this pamphlet will provide some much-needed ammunition for the fight.

Douglas A. Hyde

References to the works of Marx, Engels and Lenin are to the English translations published by Lawrence and Wishart Ltd., except The Condition of the Working Class, *which is published by Allen and Unwin Ltd.*

Many Communists are likeable, intelligent, and sincere people. They became Communists because they genuinely desired a better world, they are fired with enthusiasm for their cause and with a great hatred of injustice.

Yet the Catholic Church says that Communism and Christianity are totally incompatible, that Communism is evil, and that, in the last analysis, the struggle of our time is between the forces represented by the Catholic Church on the one hand and Communism on the other.

Is this due to bigotry on the part of the Church? Is it simply that she sees a rival and is determined to smash it?

During the course of the recent war, millions of men and women in Britain passed through our factories and millions more served in one or other of the Services. There they not infrequently met members of the Communist Party for the first time. They found them to be very different from what they had expected. They were not morons or monsters but individuals devoted to a cause and prepared to work and—if need be—sacrifice for it. But the trouble is that the cause they serve is utterly evil.

The Catholic Church has for a long time said that where you have Communism you cannot have Christianity; that when a state or individual 'goes Communist' Christianity is driven out. But many people are today bemused by the 'red haze' of pro-Soviet sentiment which swept this country after Hitler's bombers turned East in 1941; they are bemused by Communist propaganda, too, which is widespread and percolates through to all sections of the community, and such people not unnaturally feel that perhaps the Church overstates her case.

All over Europe there were people who felt like that after the war. They were Catholics who thought that they could safely co-operate with the Communists on some of their just demands. And the Communists knew how to work on such people, for they understand the modern art of propaganda and often use it to perfection.

Now, too late in some cases, those who associated with them are discovering that unless the Communists are unmasked in time, unless the influence of Communism is broken, those who assist it to power are quickly put aside and persecuted once the Communists are actually in power.

It happened in Rumania, in Hungary, and in Czecho-Slovakia, and those Catholics who thought that they could 'use' the Communists or co-operate with them discovered that the process is rather like going for a ride on a tiger—and the consequences are identical.

And just as it happened in Eastern Europe, so it could happen here.

The way to counteract the spread of Communism is to be well-informed about it. It is not sufficient simply to say that Communism is atheistic, immoral, brutal, and evil, if you have no evidence to back it up. Because almost certainly someone will turn round and say that he or she has worked with Communists and found them to be likeable, intelligent, and sincere. It is necessary to know why such people can none the less be working for an utterly evil cause and to understand something of the theory and practice of that evil cause itself. If we know *why* Communism destroys the soul and does not even make for material human happiness, we shall all the more effectively be able successfully to combat it.

But first let us remember that there is nothing to be gained by dishonest anti-Communist propaganda, founded on lies and distortions. The most effective case against Communism is the true one—and the case against Communism is damning enough to require no flights of the imagination to make it appear even worse. Let our weapons in the fight against it be truth, understanding, and Christian action.

It is the purpose of this pamphlet to provide the background for the first two in particular, along with evidence which shows how correct are the Church's allegations against it.

Let us take some of these allegations and see how far they are justified.

First, the one which has been made over and over again: Communism is atheistic and seeks to destroy all belief in God. There are some who may feel that this is somewhat far-fetched; that the first part of the above allegation may be true but that the latter assertion does not necessarily follow.

A man may, it might be argued, himself be an atheist without therefore wishing to work by every means at his disposal for the destruction of all belief in God on the part of others. But that is one of the things which distinguishes the Communist's materialism from the earlier 'free-thinker's' variety. For Communism doesn't simply say, 'There is no God'; it goes on to say, 'Men everywhere must be made to cease believing in Him'.

At the conclusion of almost every Communist meeting and demonstration, members of the crowd take off their hats and sing the 'Internationale', and when they sing the words, 'No saviours from on high deliver, no trust have we in prince or peer', they are not just singing words which they know to be empty and meaningless. On the contrary, they sum up the Marxist materialist philosophy, and the Communist sings them with the utmost conviction. For the whole Marxist case is built up on the foundation of the most militant atheism of all time, dialectical or historical materialism as it was called by its originators, Karl Marx and Friedrich Engels. That materialism is not just one odd, unimportant part of the Communist doctrine, it is its foundation upon which the entire superstructure of Communist theory and practice is built up.

It declares that everything in the universe is material, in content and in cause, from the tiniest primitive cell to the human brain itself. The mind, the will, are but material functions of that purely material grey-matter. There is, of course, no place for soul or spirit or God in such a theory. Progress and development, says the Marxist, are the result of a never-ending conflict between opposites—the dialectic from which dialectical materialism takes its name.

But let us choose, more or less at random, what the Marxist theorists themselves have had to say on the question. In his book, *Anti-Duhring* (p. 346), Engels says:

'All religion, however, is nothing but the fantastic reflection in men's minds of those external forces which control their daily life.'

On page 32 of the same book he says:

'The economic structure of society always forms the real basis from which, in the last analysis, is to be explained the whole superstructure of legal and political institutions as well as the religious, philosophical, and other conceptions of each historical period.'

Karl Marx himself summed up their view on religion when he declared that 'religion is the opium of the people'.

Lenin, who applied the teachings of Marx and Engels to the conditions of our own time—and incidentally applied them in practice too, by leading the Russian revolution—developed Marx's phrase and declared: 'Religion is a kind of spiritual intoxicant, in which slaves of capital drown their humanity and blunt their desire for a decent human existence'.

After the October revolution in Russia, Lenin had Marx's phrase engraved on the walls of the former City Hall in Moscow, right opposite the famous shrine of the Iberian Virgin Mother. Later the shrine was removed but the slogan remained.

But, it may be argued, this does not prove that Communists consciously use their dialectical materialism in their political campaigns and in their everyday lives. Here is what Engels said about dialectical materialism:

'It is our best working tool and sharpest weapon'—*Ludwig Feuerbach* (p. 54).

And that is what the Communist Party everywhere believes today.

Large numbers of people join the Communist Party here in Britain every year. Usually they are induced to become members after they have been drawn into one of the Party's campaigns on humanitarian, industrial, or quite limited political issues. They may join as a result of an emotional appeal to do so made by a Communist speaker at a great demonstration. They will almost certainly know little about Marxism and nothing about dialectical materialism.

But they will quickly learn. First, they are asked to attend a beginners' course of classes where the barest elements of Marxism are served up in highly sugar-coated form. This will be followed by a course entitled 'Scientific Socialism', which is, in fact, the elements of historical materialism—or dialectical materialism applied to history.

Soon the beginner will be 'conditioned' to a point where he himself wants to know more about 'dialectics'. And the information will, of course, be given him, probably in the shape of Stalin's classic work on the subject and in more study classes. In the process he will lose whatever religious beliefs he possessed (or go out of the Party in time) and gain an entirely new approach to all moral and ethical questions.

So the dialectical materialism of Marx is not something dead or inconsequential. It is very much alive. It is being continuously injected into people's minds here in Britain and is, of course, the official 'religion' as taught in all schools and universities throughout one-sixth of the world, namely the U.S.S.R.

The ultimate aim of the Communists is to destroy the last vestige of belief in God from the face of the earth. Any compromise or apparent easing of their anti-God campaign is no more than a purely temporary tactic designed to achieve more quickly and thoroughly that final goal.

IS IT IMMORAL?

With militant materialism as its basis it is not surprising that Communism is dishonest in all its methods, rejecting all Christian ethics and resulting in Communists themselves quickly becoming utterly unprincipled in their personal and social relationships.

But it is not simply that these are the results of the absence of good in its theories. Communist teachings on questions of ethics and principles are actively evil. Communists have a code of behaviour which determines their actions and gives them clear guidance on all major and minor questions of ethics. It is the exact opposite of that of Christianity. In *Ludwig Feuerbach* (p. 55), Engels says that when one accepts dialectical materialism:

'...the demand for final solutions and eternal truths ceases once and for all. On the other hand, one no longer permits oneself to be imposed upon by the antithesis... between true and false, good and bad...one knows that these antitheses have only relative validity'.

Marxist theory tells the Communists that the goal of socialism will be achieved only by revolution, that all 'progress' proceeds from class struggle. For the Communist that struggle is a war—and in war, he argues, any course of action is permissible. One must use correct strategy and tactics if the war is to be won. In war one employs guile and subterfuge; one seeks to penetrate the enemy's camp by stealth, outwit him, deceive him, and, if necessary, ultimately destroy him.

Before deciding on any course of action, therefore, either personal or political, the Communist has only to ask himself, 'Does it serve the class struggle?' If it does, then it is justified and no other moral or ethical considerations matter at all. If it does not, it is wrong.

Thus, for example, the British Communist Party may for a period woo the support of Liberals, Labour Party members, or some other political grouping. Or, maybe, it will seek the support of religious denominations or certain religious leaders. Or, again, some particular section of the community such as the small traders, professional classes, or intelligentsia. It will flatter them, support some of their demands in return for a measure of agreement on some point on which the Party is for the moment concentrating.

But no informed Communist will have any illusions about such an alliance. The art of winning allies and making use of them is expounded at length in the writings of Lenin and Stalin. When the end has been served they will quickly throw their allies overboard and, in the event of the Communist Party coming to power, will not hesitate to 'liquidate' them. Even whilst they use them they despise them.

Christian organizations are not infrequently used in this way. During the Spanish Civil War, for example, many Protestant clergy appeared on platforms with Communist speakers during what were, in fact, Communist campaigns. The Party used the support and standing of the clergy whilst having no illusions about what would happen to them and their religion should Communism ever come to Britain.

In Hungary in 1947 the Communists, wishing to break the resistance to the spread of their doctrine on the part of the Catholic peasantry, raised teams of volunteers to go out into the countryside each week-end repairing war-damaged Catholic churches. Communist leaders appeared in the churches when the job was done and were often garlanded by grateful congregations. Having thus won the Catholics' support and admiration they were free to seize power—which they did, and within a few months the persecution of the Church began.

Such practices are normal to Communism. Deceit is, in fact, made an art, and is studied with care by those who use it. Thus Lenin, instructing Communist journalists on their methods of work, drew their attention to the deceit and lies of sections of the 'bourgeois' press and even urged them not only to emulate them but to do the job better, studying such methods and improving upon them.

And those instructions by Lenin are printed and circulated for the use of *The Daily Worker* staff here in Britain for their guidance too.

So in their personal relations Communists will stoop

to anything provided that it 'serves the class struggle', for everything is subordinate to that.

And of personal behaviour under Marxian socialism Engels says, in his *Origin of the Family* (p. 90):

'When these people are in the world, they will care precious little what anybody today thinks they ought to do; they will make their own practice and their corresponding public opinion about the practice of each individual—and that will be the end of it.'

But, we are sometimes told, there is a new Communist morality which is higher than any 'bourgeois' morality. If we examine it we shall discover that Communism is essentially immoral. Its aim is ultimately to destroy marriage and the family as we know them today. In practice even now its influence leads to the spread of immorality and the corruption of Christian youth.

First, let us see what the Marxist theorists have said on the question, since their works are studied and applied with such devotion by the Communists themselves.

The Family.—In the *Origin of the Family* (p. 60) Engels describes the family as 'that compound of sentimentality and domestic strife', and throughout their writings, Marx and Engels advanced the view that bourgeois marriage is no more than 'legalized prostitution'.

Divorce.—On page 75 of the *Origin of the Family* Engels declares:

'Probably the only reason why the Catholic Church

17

abolished divorce was because it had convinced itself that there is no more a cure for adultery than there is for death.'

Reviewing the consequences of women working in industry, he notes with approval (p. 77) that:

'The wife has, in fact, regained the right to dissolve marriage, and if two people cannot get on with one another, they prefer to separate.'

As to divorce under Marxian socialism, he says (p. 89):

'If affection definitely comes to an end or is supplanted by a new passionate love, separation is a benefit for both partners as well as for society—only people will then be spared having to wade through the useless mire of a divorce case.'

The Home.—Looking forward to the Marxist State, Engels (p. 89) describes the 'home' as it would exist. He says:

'Private housekeeping is transformed into a social industry. The care and education of the children becomes a public affair; society looks after all children alike whether they are legitimate or not. This removes all the anxiety about the "consequences", which today is the most essential social—and moral as well as economic— factor that prevents a girl from giving herself completely to the man she loves. Will not that suffice to bring about the gradual growth of unconstrained sexual intercourse and with it a more tolerant public opinion in regard to a maiden's honour and a woman's shame?'

Woman in the Home.—'The modern individual family', he says (p. 79), 'is founded on the open or concealed domestic slavery of the wife.'

Morality.—Morality, the Marxist theorists are agreed, must be subjected only to the same test as other aspects of human behaviour. Says Lenin in his book on *Religion* (p. 56):

'For us morality is subordinated to the interests of the proletarian class struggle.' And again, on the same page: 'We say that our morality is wholly subordinated to the interests of the class struggle'.

This is reflected in practical form in the policies of the Communist Party itself and is the key to many of its campaigns. Thus, for example, the Communist Party everywhere leads the demand for more crèches and nurseries for small children, and for women to go into industry.

The woman 'comrade' who gives up her work in the office or factory to spend her time in her home and caring for her children is viewed with considerable disapproval in Party circles. The raising of the family and the moulding of children's lives upon which both the material and spiritual future of our race depends are seen as 'servitude' and a task which should be left to the State. The consequence is that the children of Communist Party members often barely know their parents and are almost totally deprived of the influence and 'atmosphere' of the home.

But the hundreds of thousands of married women who went into the factories during the war learned the appalling difficulties which face a woman with a family under such circumstances. They found, in practice, that they did not lose the 'servitude of the kitchen' but merely added to it the 'servitude' of the factory as well—for the work at home had still to be done. And today many young mothers and their infants are learning for the first time the pride and joy of parenthood and the home.

Yet the Communists must continue to campaign for the continuation of that war-time expediency since this is a fundamental of their faith.

Marxist teaching on marriage and the home was put into practical operation in Russia immediately after the revolution and the establishment of the Socialist State. Women were induced by propaganda and necessity to go into the factories and to put their children into nurseries. Abortion and divorce were made as easy as possible.

On these two last points policy has more recently been modified, but not because of any fundamental change in doctrine—that remains as before. The changes were made in the expectation of war and the need for unlimited 'cannon fodder'. For this reason large numbers of children (who are accommodated in the crèches and nurseries) were, and still are, encouraged. But this is but further proof of the utter cynicism of the Communists, for they have every intention of returning to the fundamental teachings on the question once the size of the population has been sufficiently increased. It is a degrading manifestation of the Communist practice of making millions of people order their lives like so many machines responding to the leaders at the top.

Communist teachings on morality are reflected, too, in the personal lives of Communist Party members. The sneers at bourgeois marriage, the sanctity of the marriage vows and the home, and the evil theories they are taught, inevitably have their effect on the members' personal behaviour and leave their mark on those who pass through the Party's ranks. Thousands of young men and women and sincere workers are annually corrupted as a consequence.

From the network of organizations which surround the Communist Party and are created by it, goes out an ever widening influence against all accepted Christian ideas on the home, family, children, and morality which results in a growth of cynicism and immorality in circles far removed from Communism and which are by no means Marxist.

It undermines, in fact, all those conventions which have their origins in Christian teaching and practice over a period of centuries. It represents a way of life quite unlike that which grew out of our Western Christian civilization. And although it is true that in our largely pagan England of today immorality, inverted values, and an absence of an effective ethical code are to be found among wide masses of the people, it is only in the

Communist movement that these things are elevated to a theory and practice which is set up in opposition to that of Christianity, consciously pursued in an organized way.

Communists are the most active of propagandists, constantly seeking to spread their influence and increase their numbers. But they do not hope ever to win a majority by persuasion and propaganda, neither would they be prepared to wait for the completion of that process even though they thought it might in time be achieved.

The whole of Communist hopes for the achievement of power are dependent upon the use of violence as a means of imposing a system of Communism upon an unwilling and unprepared majority. Their aim is, not to win a majority, but to build up a hard, reliable core of determined supporters who, by superior organization and strategy, can exploit a difficult situation when it arises.

This is how power was achieved in Russia and the process has, since the war, been repeated many times in the countries of Eastern Europe. There the presence of the Red Army and the opportunity to 'deal with' many of the Communists' opponents during the war itself, by means of the resistance movements and, later, purges of 'collaborators', reduced the violence at the time of the seizure of power to a minimum. But those conditions are recognized as peculiar ones, unlikely to occur again except by means of Soviet warlike 'expansion'.

Elsewhere 'heavy' revolution on the lines of the Russian model is anticipated and prepared for.

Following the usual tactics, however, the Communists use parliamentary institutions and democratic organizations for the pursuit of their aims whilst having nothing but contempt for them and every intention of abolishing them at the earliest possible moment.

Harry Pollitt, the British leader, has many times, on the radio and elsewhere, claimed that 'Communism is simply Socialism in its working clothes'. This is one of those 'homely' meaningless phrases which the Communists use so successfully to deceive the unsuspecting. On the face of it, it appears, in so far as it means anything at all, to suggest that this is just a working-class version of something with which we are already familiar and which is accepted as part of our democracy. But we should not be taken in by such phrases.

The whole theory of Marxism builds up to the need for revolutionary action and on this the leading writers are quite specific. Said Lenin in his book, *What is to be Done?* (p. 28); also quoted by Stalin in *Foundations of Leninism:*

'Without a revolutionary theory there can be no revolutionary movement.'

And that is the main goal of all the Communists' theorizing and practical activities.

Karl Marx, in *The German Ideology* (p. 69), wrote:

'This revolution is necessary, therefore, not only because the ruling class cannot be overthrown in any other way, but also because the class *overthrowing* it can only in a revolution succeed in ridding itself of all the muck of the ages and become fitted to found society anew.'

What sort of society is intended we have already seen.

And so each of the leading Marxist theorists has written at length on the theory and practice of insurrection, or as Engels and, later, Lenin called it, 'the art of insurrection'. Works by these writers in which the guiding principles are clearly laid down are published by the Communist Party publishers in this country and sold in numbers to their sympathizers. They are studied with great care, and education courses are based upon them in which all Party members are expected to participate. The lessons learned from the failure of the Paris Commune in 1871 and the success of the October Revolution in Russia in 1917 are learned by heart and kept ready for the day when they may be applied here in Britain and throughout the world.

In *The Condition of the Working Class* (p. 296), Engels declared:

'The war of the poor against the rich will be the bloodiest ever waged.'

And Marx, in *The Poverty of Philosophy* (p. 147), said:

'Combat or death; bloody struggle or extinction. It is thus that the question is inexorably put.'

And after the revolution, what then?

There have, after all, been other ideals that men have thought worth shedding blood for. Communism, too, claims to be an ideal. It fights, it says, on behalf of the working-class who are the majority class in any modern society. According to the Communist leaders and pamphleteers, its purpose is to end the exploitation of man by man, introduce social and economic justice at last, and establish a classless society. May it not be that such ends justify the means?

It is by reasoning in this way that many people find themselves inside the Party. But there is a vast gulf between the slogans and the reality. Between the braided dictators of the Eastern European countries and the common people lies a vast gulf and the Communist parties of those countries, far from bridging it, simply widen it as time goes on and the Communist leadership becomes more and more entrenched as a class apart.

The so-called 'dictatorship of the proletariat' is in fact a dictatorship of the Communist Party, and, because of the way in which it is organized, that in turn narrows down to a dictatorship of the four or five who constitute the Party's political bureau.

The form of organization employed by the Communist Parties of the world is known as 'centralized democracy', but it has nothing to do with democracy as it is known and practised elsewhere. Its methods of election and determining of policy are the exact reverse of that which obtains in genuinely democratic organizations. Instead of policies being determined by the membership and imposed upon the leaders, the opposite obtains. Policy is decided by the political bureau, which is made up of a handful of the top leaders. They then see that the policy is endorsed by the larger executive committee. 'Leads' and directives are then handed down to the district and branch committees.

There is considerable discussion at every level—but it is within the well-defined limits set by the original political bureau recommendations and usually turns on their local application rather than on their content. A branch finding itself in disagreement with the main line of the Party may express its point of view at Annual Congress but, if defeated, must then accept the majority decision as absolutely binding. If it persists in raising the question again it will find itself dissolved, with its leaders expelled. This happened quite recently in the case of a branch of the British Party, So that, in practice, the very few individuals who make up the political bureau are all-powerful on policy questions.

So far as their position in the organization is concerned, they are in an equally strong position. Instead of elections coming through nominations from 'below', the 'panels' method is employed. Nominations are accepted from the branches and district committees prior to Annual Congress, but the political bureau itself selects a full list of those whom it would like to see constituting the

Executive Committee and presents the names as a 'panel' to the Executive Committee for endorsement. Then, at Congress, a small 'panels commission' is set up, led by a member of the political bureau and filled with 'reliable' comrades. The branch nominees and those of the executive are considered by the commission. The panel of names put forward will be accepted in whole or with only the slightest of alterations and then put before Congress for endorsement as a whole—not individually. Congress can in theory reject them but again it must reject the list as a whole. In practice it, of course, accepts, and the people selected by the political bureau then constitute the new Executive Committee who proceed to *appoint* the new bureau—which means that they re-appoint the existing one.

Thus the Communist Party leader is in an almost unshakable position, provided that he plays ball with the other leaders. And if and when his party captures power he inevitably becomes one of the tiny ruling clique with a power greater than any ruling monarch ever enjoyed in the past.

Kruschev in Russia, Tito in Yugoslavia, Mao in China—these men have a power such as has never been known among rulers before—and they are all the stronger for the fact that they have a disciplined party of zealots supporting them and believing that by their 'centralized democracy' they are controlling them.

So it is that the achievement of power by the Communists means the destruction of democracy and of personal liberty. Behind the slogans and the shouting is the cold science of Marxism, concerned, not with human beings as such, but with the establishment of a guinea-pig world based on the anti-religious, soulless teachings of Marx and Engels.

Does it serve the cause of Communism? That is the only consideration. The individual Communist in the State counts for nothing, yet by skilful propaganda, education in dialectical materialism, and terrorism where necessary, he can be brought to believe that he is participating in a great experiment in which he has a part to play and responsibilities to fulfil. So it is that decisions can be made and operated which will blight the lives of hundreds of thousands, and the party membership, at least, will believe the suffering involved to be justified because it 'serves the cause'. Thus entire populations can be uprooted and shifted to another part or dispersed throughout the land to serve some tactical political consideration. When Tito's Government in Yugoslavia found it impossible to destroy an armed opposition which was functioning in the mountain areas the entire populations of towns and villages were moved out and scattered throughout the land in order to destroy the guerrillas' base.

In the U.S.S.R., areas occupied by the Nazis suffered appalling devastation as the war swung to and fro across them. The people were subjected to the worst of humiliations and cruelties by the invading Germans. But at the conclusion of the war the Russian leaders took the view that the population of such areas was likely to have been corrupted by 'bourgeois' influences during the occupation and so, after all the horrors they had already endured, they were torn up by their roots from the places which had been their homes and sent east to the vast, under-populated areas of Siberia where they can do no harm.

Such decisions, appalling in their tragic human consequences, are normal to Communism and can be fully justified according to Marxist standards, for, it can be argued, the victims suffer that the cause of Communism may prevail.

The utter abandonment of all ideas about the sanctity of the individual, which is a feature of Christian teaching, leads inevitably to such consequences.

IS IT INEVITABLE?

Half a dozen countries of Europe have now fallen to the Communists. Communism knocks at the door of several others. China, Mongolia, Manchuria, Korea, North Vietnam, are already Communist. In 1848 Karl Marx in his Communist Manifesto, wrote: 'A spectre is haunting Europe, the spectre of Communism…let the ruling classes tremble'. It was largely wishful thinking on his part then. Today it is a reality. Communism is haunting the world. But it is not just the ruling classes who tremble. The working-class in the conquered and threatened countries tremble too, for they are learning that Communism means tyranny, the destruction of personal liberty, and the end of all those Christian values which in the past we have taken for granted but which are the basis of our way of life. There can, therefore, be no question of the end justifying the means, for they are equally evil.

Here in Britain Communism is not numerically strong. Membership of the Communist Party has never been above 60,000 and has often been much less. But more than 10,000 members pass through its ranks each year and several thousands more through the Young Communist League, and in doing so lose their faith and accept new, cynical, inverted standards.

And the Party's influence is vastly in excess of its numerical strength. This is partly because of its form of organization and its hold on leading positions in the trade union and Labour movement, but still more because of the devotion and energy of its members.

A number of the most important trade unions have Communists in their leadership and almost all unions have an overweighting of Communists in responsible positions at district and branch levels. Those positions have, first and foremost, been obtained because of the readiness to accept responsibility and to do the most routine and least-sought-after jobs where necessary.

Membership of the appropriate trade union and co-operative society is made a condition of membership of the Party and members are taught that they must be the best possible members of those organizations. The result is that Communists everywhere tend to be elected to positions of responsibility and quickly move up the ladder from one level to the next. That process is at times accelerated by the aid of 'packed' meetings and even by subterfuge, but far more often it is due to the energy of the Communists and the apathy of non-Communists. It could quickly be brought to an end by an increased sense of responsibility on the part of their opponents and, in particular, Catholics who are aware of the real danger of Communism and the urgent need to defeat it. Vigilance and energy on the part of such organizations as the Association of Catholic Trade Unionists could break the Communist hold on our Labour movement in a very short time.

But out-manoeuvring the Communists will not be enough if the victory is to be a lasting one. The greater sense of responsibility and willingness to give time and work to such organizations will require to be an enduring one or the pertinacity of the Communists will again prevail.

And the same may be said of all those other organizations which the Communists have captured or penetrated—student bodies, tenants' organizations, co-operative societies, sections of the Labour Party, cultural organizations, the factory organizations of the workers and so on.

The strength of the Communist Party lies in the zeal of its members, for whom no sacrifice is too great, no job too hard. Fired with enthusiasm for the teachings which are for them their religion, they put Christians and non-Communists to shame. Their success is a measure of our failure to make the same sacrifice for a better cause, and to the extent to which we see this and act upon it shall we defeat them.

COMMUNISM AND THE HOME

Douglas Hyde

COMMUNISM AND THE HOME

Douglas A Hyde

When the Catholic Church attacks Communism it does not do so on political grounds. It warns against it and attempts to counter the spread of its influence in every possible way because it is atheistic, immoral and degrading to man. Its ideas, says the Church, are false and must by their very nature bring with them great unhappiness. And nowhere is this more true than in the case of the home and family.

But, precisely because Catholics have been in the forefront of the fight against Communism, may it not be that the Church has got a distorted picture of its aims? May it not be that the Popes and priests who have denounced it have been, even with the best of intentions, too prejudiced to give a fair interpretation of it?

If we compare what the Church has had to say on Communism and the family with what the Communist leaders and thinkers themselves have said, coupled with the knowledge of Communism in practice which we now have, we shall be in a position to judge for ourselves.

In his Encyclical letter *Divini Redemptoris*, Pope Pius XI had this to say under the heading, 'Marriage and family under Communism':

'In a system which thus scorns and rejects all the sacred functions of human life it follows as a matter of course that matrimony and the family are considered to be a purely civil and artificial institution, originating in a particular set of economic conditions, and as the theory refuses to recognize any matrimonial bond of the juridical and moral order not completely dependent on the will of the individual or the community, it likewise and as a necessary consequence denies the indissoluble perpetuity of wedlock.

'The complete emancipation of woman from any ties with home or family is a special characteristic of the Communist theory. Held to be totally free from the protective authority of her husband, the wife is withdrawn from the home and the care of her children and, equally with her husband, thrust into the turmoil of public life and communal industry, her home and children being handed over to the custody of the State. Parents, finally, are denied the right to educate their offspring; this right is claimed exclusively for the community and is therefore allowed to be exercised only in its name and by its mandate.'

I do not think that the Marxist position has ever been stated more plainly or more accurately and in so few words.

But it is, of course, very different to the picture which is given us by Communist propagandists to-day.

For they know that their theories, stated starkly and in such a way, would attract no one, least of all members of the working class to whom they make their special appeal, and whose lives have always centred around the home.

It is only in the Communists' theoretical works, published for their own study and enlightenment, that the real position is to be found.

The Individual

Since the family, like the community, is made up of individuals and will succeed only in so far as the individual worth of each is recognized, let us see first how the individual would fare under Communism.

We need have no doubt about this aspect of Marxist teaching for it has been stated with the utmost clarity and frankness in a book called *The ABC of Communism*, which was published by the Communist Party of Great Britain itself in 1922.

That was at a time when few besides the Communists read their books and when the party's aims were in any case still discussed by them in public. In 1934 an international decision was taken to pursue quite different tactics and Communists all over the world switched over to 'popularizing' their case for public consumption and never stating it frankly—whilst at the same time continuing to study their true aims in private.

But even in the franker days of 1922 *The ABC of Communism* was felt to be the type of thing which should, if possible, be kept in party members' hands, and so it was published by the party itself. Every party leader still has his copy, for it is a fundamental work, but it is no longer on public sale.

On page 242 of this book we read:

'When parents say, "My daughter", "my son", the words do not simply imply the existence of a parental relationship, they also give expression to the parents' view that they have a right to educate their own children. From the Socialist outlook, no such right exists. The individual human being does not belong to himself, but to society, to the human race. The individual can only live and thrive owing to the existence of society. The child, therefore, belongs to the society in which it lives and thinks, to which it came into being—and this society is something wider than the "society" of its own parents.'

That makes the position abundantly clear. Under Communism—'the individual does not belong to himself, but to society'—or, if you like, the State.

That is not an attractive proposition for we know to-day how easily 'society' can overlook the individual. 'Society' thinks in terms of the masses, of millions, and the sacred worth of the individual counts for little in a super card-index system.

Why do the Communists hold such an unattractive theory? If you think about it, the reason is clear.

Communism is atheistic. It denies the existence of God—indeed it aims to erase the very memory of the name of God from the minds of men and believes that it cannot triumph until it has done so.

But if man does not belong to God, is not answerable to Him for his behaviour, to whom is he answerable?

'He does not belong to himself,' the Marxists anxiously assert. For if he did he would be answerable only to himself. He could determine his own course of action regardless of right or wrong; permissible or not permissible. No state could tolerate such a position. You could not rule men who recognized no restraints, human or Divine, in a Communist state any more than in any other.

And so 'society' is made to take the place of God. What is right and what is wrong is laid down by the Communist State. The individual's rights are what are permitted him by the State. Outside that he has no rights whatsoever.

And you can see where that leads in practice in the countries of Eastern Europe to-day. Nowhere on earth does the individual count for so little. The State is all-powerful and the individual who is unable or who refuses to accept its ruling hopes for little mercy from it.

That is the background to the millions of people in the forced-labour camps, the hundreds of thousands in the jails, the thousands of people who have fled to other lands because their lives were endangered by the mere fact that they were known to hold views contrary to those of the men who use the State as their repressive weapon to-day. It is the meaning of the imprisonment of Cardinal Stepinac and Cardinal Mindszenty.

The individual, then, belongs to the State, according to Communist reasoning.

The Family

But individuals marry, and have families. What has Communism to say about marriage?

Christian marriage, based on an indissoluble union between man and wife, was always subject to derision on the part of Marx and Engels, the founders of modern Communism. It had, they claimed, failed. 'Bourgeois marriage is in reality a system of wives in common,' they said on page 25 of the *Communist Manifesto*. And their disciple August Bebel wrote in *Woman, Past, Present and Future:*

> '... it follows as a matter of course that our modern marriage is very far from fulfilling its true purpose and has therefore no claim to be regarded as either sacred or moral.' (Page 49).

> 'The only salvation lies in a return to nature and to natural intercourse between the sexes, in casting off the unhealthy, spiritualistic ideas of humanity which cling to us to-day.' (Page 70).

The mother, busy in the home about her responsible household tasks, undertaking the huge but magnificently satisfying job of rearing the children, they saw as a slave who should be emancipated.

Marx, incidentally, employed a nurse-housekeeper even throughout the frequent periods when he was dependent upon outside charity. In this way he assisted in the 'emancipation' of his own wife whilst passing on the 'slavery' to someone else.

The woman who makes looking after the home and bringing up the children a full-time job is economically dependent upon her husband, they declared, for they did not see it as a partnership but as the exploitation of one by the other.

By going into industry and earning her own 'keep' the woman would be freed. Freed from 'economic dependence' upon her husband; freed to do everything he did; freed from having to stick to him for life, and able to support herself should she prefer to dissolve the marriage.

In an age lacking a sense of responsibility and of distorted values it has had a wide appeal. At one time, in the days when the whole of life was based on Christian precepts, it would have sounded monstrous.

Holding such views the Communists everywhere campaign to get women out of the home and into the factory.

In the Communist countries they are subjected to considerable pressure in order to get them there. Day nurseries, creches, communal restaurants in flats and factories are provided for this purpose. The aim is that every woman should be in industry and every child out of the home.

Frederick Engels wrote a book called *Origin of the Family* which is the classic work on this subject. Every serious Marxist possesses it and studies it. Upon it has been based most of the legislation passed on the home and family in the Communist countries.

On page 80 he says:

> 'Then it will be plain that the first condition for the liberation of the wife is to bring the whole female sex into public industry, and that this in turn demands the abolition of the monogamous family as the economic unit of society.'

And on page 77 we find him declaring that when the woman goes into the factory:

> 'The wife has in fact regained the right to dissolve marriage and if two people cannot get on together they prefer to separate.'

Woman's place under Communism would not, therefore, any longer be in the home but in the factory. And her job as wife and mother would not be seen as one of the most satisfying and important of all, but a form of slavery from which she must be emancipated.

The Children

And how about the children? We have already seen that the newly-born infant would not be regarded as the priceless possession of the parents, to be dedicated to God, but rather as the property of society. And so it is not surprising that the parents' right to train and mould their children's minds is seen, not only as something undesirable, but as something to be resisted at all costs. Which is logical enough, of course, if they are the property of the State. Parents would mould and make individuals. The Communist State needs robots.

On page 262 of *The ABC of Communism* we find the position stated clearly:

> 'The decree whereby the school is separated from the church must be rigidly enforced, and the proletarian state must not make the slightest concession to medievalism. What has already been done to throw off the yoke of religion is all too little, for it still remains within the power of ignorant parents to cripple the minds of their children by teaching them religious fables.
>
> 'We must see to it that the school assumes the offensive against religious propaganda in the homes so that from the very outset the children's minds shall

be rendered immune to all those religious fairy tales which many grown-ups continue to regard as truth.'

And also on the same page:

'Under the Soviet Power there is freedom of conscience for adults. But this freedom of conscience for parents is tantamount to a freedom for them to poison the minds of their children with the opium which when they were young was poured into their own minds by the church. The parents force upon the children their own dullness, their own ignorance; they proclaim as truth all sorts of nonsense; and they thus greatly increase the difficulties which the unified labour schools have to encounter. One of the most important tasks of the proletarian state is to liberate children from the reactionary influence exercised by their parents.'

And the *Communist Manifesto*, page 25, says:

'Do you charge us with wanting to stop the exploitation of children by their parents? To this crime we plead guilty.'

In Russia and elsewhere it has resulted in an appalling separation between children and parents. The fight for the 'liberation of children from the influence of their parents' has had its logical end in children having the right to prosecute their parents for administering punishment to them and in the child-spies who have denounced their parents to the secret police and have been extolled for doing so.

In seeking to gain a complete hold on the mind of the rising generation the State has had to combat and destroy the influence—particularly the Christian influence—of the parent in the home. Only so can it be certain that the men and women of to-morrow will be wholly subject to it and wholly possessed by it.

The School

And what about the schools? Having gone to such trouble to possess the infant's mind and soul it is natural that the Communist State should have very definite views on what is permissible and what not permissible in the realm of education.

First, of course, it is laid down that only the State, and not the parents, shall decide how and where the child is to be educated.

In *The ABC of Communism* it is put like this:

> 'To society, likewise, belongs a primary and basic right of educating children. From this point of view the parents' claim to bring up their own children, and thereby to impress upon the children's psychology their own limitations, must not merely be rejected, but must be absolutely laughed out of court. Society may entrust the education of children to the parents; but it may refuse to do anything of the kind,

and there is all the more reason why society should refuse to entrust education to the parents seeing that the faculty of educating children is far more rarely encountered than the faculty of begetting them.' (Page 242).

And the education provided will be based on dialectical materialism. All religious teaching is dropped.

Said *The ABC of Communism:*

"We must ruthlessly expel from the proletarian school all those teachers of the old schools who either cannot or will not become instruments for the Communist enlightenment of the masses…The old school was intimately associated with religion—by compulsory religious teaching, compulsory attendance at prayers and compulsory church going. The new school forcibly expels religion from within its walls under whatever guise it seeks entry and in whatever diluted form reactionary groups of parents may desire to drag it back again.' (Pages 239-40).

That was the issue which Cardinal Mindszenty saw so clearly and for which he was prepared to be martyred. He knew that once the Communist State got hold of the educational system it would use all its persuasive and coercive powers to produce a generation of militant atheists.

Lenin, the architect of the Russian revolution, and

the greatest of modern Marxist theorists, laid it down in these words:

'The fight against religion, the opium of the people, occupies an important position among the tasks of the cultural revolution. This fight must be carried on persistently and systematically. The proletarian power must withdraw all State support from the Church, and abolish the influence exercised by the Church, on the system of education and training organized by the State; it must ruthlessly suppress the counter-revolutionary activities of ecclesiastical organizations.

'The proletarian power acknowledges freedom of conscience, but at the same time uses all the means at its disposal to conduct anti-religious propaganda, abolishes the privileged position of the established church and reforms the entire educational system on the basis of the scientific materialist conception of the world.' (*Lenin on Religion*, page 9.)

So, by controlling the child's thought from the cradle to manhood, the Communists hope in time to have a generation which believes unquestioningly all that it is told, which has never known anything of the Faith its fathers held and which is incapable of seeing beyond its intellectual and spiritual prison-house. But what about what is left of married life?

With mother in the factory, children in the hands of the State, what happens to marriage as an institution?

Engels' book *The Origin of the Family* sets out to show that modern marriage belongs to an earlier, more primitive period in man's development. And Marxists have always held that under Communism both marriage and divorce must be as easy as possible.

Said August Bebel in *Woman, Past, Present and Future:*

'The gratification of the sexual impulse is as strictly the personal affair of the individual as the gratification of every other natural instinct. No one has to give an account of him or herself, and no third person has the slightest right of intervention…Should incompatibility, disappointment and dislike ensue, morality demands the dissolution of the tie that has become unnatural and therefore immoral.' (Pages 229-30).

And Engels in *Origin of the Family*, page 89, uses very similar words:

'If affection definitely comes to an end or is supplanted by a new passionate love, separation is a benefit for both partners as well as for society—only people will then be spared having to wade through the useless mire of a divorce case.'

He adds:

'Probably the only reason why the Catholic Church abolished divorce was because it has convinced itself that there is no more a cure for adultery than there is for death.' (Page 75).

'Easy come, easy go', will therefore be the rule under Communism. There is nothing sacred where there is no God. Marriage is no longer sacred, the marriage act is robbed of its spirituality, parenthood is shorn of its sacred responsibility. So why be faithful, why be chaste, why stick together at all?

Legislation aimed at carrying the Marxist ideas on the home and family into effect was passed in Russia soon after the revolution.

Any church marriage could be declared null and void; state marriage became the easiest possible, divorce could be obtained by either party sending a postcard to the local registrar's office in return for which another card was sent officially declaring the marriage at an end.

Under the circumstances large numbers did not bother to observe such meaningless formalities either when establishing or dissolving their 'homes'.

Abortion was made legal, abortion clinics were set up all over the country and considerable propaganda done to encourage their use.

Such clinics were necessary if large numbers of unwanted children were not to result from the temporary attachments which became prevalent throughout the land.

The consequences were such that within 16 years the security and survival of the State itself were threatened.

On July 12, 1936, *Izvestia* reported that in Moscow province in 1934, 57,000 children were born, while 154,000 abortions were performed. In the villages there were 242,979 births to 324,194 abortions.

And the same official paper, on July 4, 1935, reported that in the same province in the first five months of the year, there were 38% more divorces than registered marriages. About 2.3% of divorced couples, it said, had children and only 10% of such divorced parents could support them.

The Russian leaders were by this time convinced that war with the West was almost inevitable and that perhaps a whole series of wars might be expected until the issue between Communism and Capitalism was settled internationally once and for all.

Russia's great asset in war had traditionally been her large population. Cannon fodder in almost unlimited quantities would, therefore, be needed in the future. But the state of affairs depicted in the *Izvestia* reports was one in which it was clear that such cannon fodder would soon no longer be available. More births and less abortions, and stable homes in which children were born were needed.

And so, with typical Communist flexibility, the line was changed.

The legislation of 1918 and 1927 was rescinded. Divorce became more difficult and was discouraged. Abortion was made an offence. Large families were encouraged. For the time being part of Communist practice was put into cold storage. Party members were told that this new attitude did not represent a denial of the Marxist principles on the question. It was a necessary expedient forced upon the Soviet State by the threats of a hostile capitalist world and by the fact that the masses had not been educated 'up' to Marxist practice.

A period in which there was a conscious retreat was necessary until, by means of a better understanding of the teachings of Engels, the masses were ready for the 'emancipation' which was the Communist goal. Such 'theoretical' retreats are a normal feature of Communism in practice as witness the 'retreat' from Communism to the New Economic Policy of March 1921, when Communism was deliberately put into cold storage for the time being.

To ensure that the party members themselves should not come in time to believe their own propaganda in favour of the home and family, new emphasis was placed upon the need for the study and understanding of Marxist theory. All over the world Communists still stand by the theory; it has not been modified, or revised or amended in any way whatsoever. But it is not discussed in public to-day. It is reserved for the party study class, for practice in the Communists' own personal life—and for the future.

In China, in 1934, when only one-eighth of that country had been made Soviet, a constitution and set of 'Fundamental Laws of the Chinese Soviet Republic' were

51

drawn up. After party leaders everywhere had been given the opportunity of acquiring copies and understanding what would be the constitution of the Soviet China of the future, they were withdrawn. But it was made clear in the preamble that these would become the operative laws when the whole of China had been Sovietised. They, too, were based on Marxist thought, for the Chinese Communists are in no way less Marxist than those of Russia or elsewhere.

Under that Constitution marriage and divorce were made as easy as possible.

Article 8 of the Regulations concerning marriage says:

> "In order to conclude a marriage the man and woman concerned shall jointly appear at the rural or town Soviet in order to register the marriage and receive the certificate of marriage.'

That is all that is required.

And on divorce, Article 9 says:

> 'There shall be freedom of divorce. A divorce may be granted with the mutual consent and at the mutual request of both husband and wife; likewise if a peremptory demand shall be made by either one of the parties.'

Article 10 explains that to obtain such a divorce it would be necessary only that 'the divorce must be registered in the rural or town Soviet.'

That Chinese draft legislation became the prototype of Communist legislation everywhere and the constitutions of the various countries which have gone Communist' since that date have been largely modelled upon it.

But Russia and China are far away. How about Britain?

British Communists have modelled their party's organization, its theory and its practice upon the Russian party, as have Communists everywhere. In the party's study courses the Marxist teaching on the home and family is learned with the same care and enthusiasm as in Russia.

The English translation of Engels' 'classic' *Origin of the Family* has a large sale in Communist circles and is used as a text-book in classes and study courses all over the country.

Morality

The British Communists' ideas on morality are based upon it and upon the other works quoted in this pamphlet—indeed the books and passages quoted here are ones used by the author of this pamphlet in study courses which he himself tutored when a Communist.

And just as Communists here accept the theories so, too, they have supported their practice.

The British Communist Party has based—and still bases—many of its campaigns upon the Marxist theories on the family. Often they appear to the general public as relatively harmless, indeed some people regard them as being among the less revolutionary of the Communists' activities.

Thus, for example, the Communist Party supports every move which will make it easier for women to go into industry and away from the home. It has led the campaigns for creches and day nurseries and gained many notable successes during the war, on this.

It has been a strong supporter of the demand for more and more British Restaurants, and has fought every attempt by the Government and local authorities to close them. Its campaigns for equal pay (whatever may be the motives of others associated in such movements) and for the recruitment of women into the mills and factories have all been aimed at paving the way psychologically and physically for the vast extension of such developments under Communism.

Communist Party members and their associates here have initiated campaigns for easier divorce, for abortion law 'reform' and anything else which was in accord with Marxist principles.

The woman who prefers to make a full time job of being a wife and mother is looked at with suspicion and contempt.

The majority of the party's leadership spent periods in Moscow or Leningrad prior to the repeal of the divorce and abortion legislation in 1936. They accepted the prevailing practices of the time—and brought them back to Britain with them. But when Russia put its practice—or some aspects of it—into cold storage the need for Communists to do so in Britain and the other capitalist countries did not arise in the same way since they had not the responsibilities of running a state. The practice therefore very largely continued here.

It is true that the party's public propaganda on the question became a little less blatant, less outrageous, but that was part of a general tactic of concealing the real aims of Communism from the public in order to facilitate the formation of Popular Fronts. But, as in Russia, side by side with the new propaganda line went intensified study of the fundamental teachings by the Communists themselves.

And, regardless of what may be their public line on the question, because Communists accept the Marxist view, their practice must almost inevitably be immoral too.

Every Communist longs for the day when he can practise his Communism. But that requires a Communist State, preceded by a civil war. And until that day comes he must continue to live in a capitalist society whether he likes it or not.

But there is one aspect of his Marxist teaching which he can commence to practise right away. And that is precisely the one we have been outlining.

As a Communist he will hate 'bourgeois' conventions. He can defy them at once in his personal life, by the practice of Engels' teachings. As an atheist no marriage vows will be binding upon him. He can break them as soon as he likes and as often as he likes. He can form temporary associations, marry and re-marry or just not bother to do so, with an easy conscience, for it is all in accord with his beliefs. And in order to avoid 'the consequences' in a state which makes no provision for such things he will campaign for, and practise, the widest possible use of contraceptives and abortions.

Even where the individual's reactions are not as positive as this his approach to marriage and sexual relations will become coloured by the views he adopts. There will, almost inevitably, be a loosening up in his personal life. One cannot habitually sneer at marriage as 'legalised prostitution', proclaim the freedom which comes from philandering, describe the marriage act as of no more significance than taking a glass of water, and regard the family as an out-worn notion without certain definite consequences in one's own life.

And so, one of the first fruits of joining the Communist Party is often the undermining of the home in the case of adult and of their morality in the case of youths.

And what has been said of the Communist Party goes equally for the Young Communist League—the party's own creation for bringing adolescents within its influence and which it officially describes as 'the school for Communism.'

The worker whose life has revolved around his home will in most cases quickly gravitate away from it. Quite probably he will begin, after years of stability, to become unstable as a husband, having 'affairs' as the rest of the local members do and before long making more serious attachments which not infrequently wreck the home.

In the case of the woman who becomes a party member the results are often more noticeable, more profound and still more devastating.

She is seen less and less in the home. She sets about escaping from 'the servitude of the kitchen'. She demonstrates her emancipation from an unjust social system by an entirely new and looser approach to the need for faithfulness in marriage. Consciously, in many cases, man and wife will agree to give each other 'freedom to wander'. And they do.

The children become a burden, interfering with party activities. Mother goes out to work. The children go into the nursery and become among the most neglected and loveless in the land.

Ten thousand people pass through the ranks of the British Communist Party each year. Ten thousand people annually are corrupted in one way or another. Very few have years in the party and come out clean.

The Communist Party attracts some of the keenest and best of our day and perverts them. And in no sphere of its activities is this more the case than in the realm of morality, the home and family.

Out from the party far and wide go corrupting influences. The ideas and practices spread by Communists appear attractive to many others, particularly youths and girls with little religious background or moral training and so are accepted by them. Such views cannot be held and practised, even for a brief period, without irrevocable consequences and life-long regrets.

Communism might be described as the sum total of all the heresies, wrong ideas and false notions that people have had for generations, exaggerated and elevated to a philosophy and a way of life.

Wrong ideas and wrong practice on questions of marriage and morality are not the exclusive possession of the Communists. The ever-growing queues at the divorce courts so soon after the 'reform' of our divorce laws are a bitter evidence of this. They are a matter, too, of growing concern, not only to Christians, but to those responsible for the stability and survival of the State itself.

The child delinquents who appear in the juvenile courts in increasing numbers include a high percentage of the victims of broken homes and divorces. Separations and unsuccessful marriages are seen as being one of the principal causes of the growth of child crime.

Just as the problem of combating modern materialism is wider than that of the fight against Marxist materialism so is it the case with the home and family. In Marxism we find materialism in its most virulent, militant organized form. So, in Marxism we find contempt for Christian morality and Christian marriage in its most virulent, militant and organized form too.

Communism in practice, precisely because it carries commonly-held but utterly wrong ideas to extremes, is demonstrating before our eyes to-day just how false these ideas have been. It is proving how their practice brings unhappiness and degradation to men, women and children alike. And if those who see where these things are wrong speak out our generation can be brought back to sanity.

For the practice of Communism is demonstrating just how right has been the Church all along and how her ideas, which are the exact opposite of those of the Marxists, have been the ones which alone are in keeping with the dignity of man.

In his first encyclical in 1939 the present Pope described domestic life as 'the primary cell of human society'. That is the Christian conception of the home and family. That way lies both sanity and sanctity.

BACKGROUND

In the aftermath of the Second World War, Communism in Britain had gained some fleeting glamour on account of the wartime alliance with Soviet Russia. There was still widespread refusal to acknowledge either the staggering mass murders perpetrated by Stalin and his gang, nor the inevitably tyrannical nature of Communist rule (then newly exercised over much of Eastern Europe). Any such reports were dismissed as prejudiced, probably inspired by reactionary elements, and obviously exaggerated (these attitudes, it might be said, are still with us). In this context, the testimony of one such as Douglas Hyde was invaluable. Hyde's background as an active Communist, his honesty about the brutal, deceiving and unscrupulous tactics used by Communism to achieve its ends, and his clear statement of what those ends were (and their manifest incompatibility with Christian morals), all went far to counterbalance what he freely admitted were the plausibility and evident sincerity of many Communists.

CTS ONEFIFTIES

1. FR DAMIEN & WHERE ALL ROADS LEAD · *Robert Louis Stevenson & G K Chesterton*

2. THE UNENDING CONFLICT · *Hilaire Belloc*

3. CHRIST UPON THE WATERS · *John Henry Newman*

4. DEATH & RESURRECTION · *Leonard Cheshire VC & Bede Jarrett OP*

5. THE DAY THE BOMB FELL · *Johannes Siemes SJ & Bruce Kent*

6. MIRACLES · *Ronald Knox*

7. A CITY SET ON A HILL · *Robert Hugh Benson*

8. FINDING THE WAY BACK · *Francis Ripley*

9. THE GUNPOWDER PLOT · *Herbert Thurston SJ*

10. NUNS – WHAT ARE THEY FOR? · *Maria Boulding OSB, Bruno Webb OSB & Jean Cardinal Daniélou SJ*

11. ISLAM, BRITAIN & THE GOSPEL · *John Coonan, William Burridge & John Wijngaards*

12. STORIES OF THE GREAT WAR · *Eileen Boland*

13. LIFE WITHIN US · *Caryll Houselander, Delia Smith & Herbert Fincham*

14. INSIDE COMMUNISM · *Douglas Hyde*

15. COURTSHIP: SOME PRACTICAL ADVICE · *Anon, Hubert McEvoy SJ, Tony Kirwin & Malcolm Brennan*

16. RESURRECTION · *Vincent McNabb OP & B C Butler OSB*

17. TWO CONVERSION STORIES · *James Britten & Ronald Knox*

18. MEDIEVAL CHRISTIANITY · *Christopher Dawson*

19. A LIBRARY OF TALES – VOL 1 · *Lady Herbert of Lea*

20. A LIBRARY OF TALES – VOL 2 · *Eveline Cole & E Kielty*

21. WAR AT HOME AND AT THE FRONT · *"A Chaplain" & Mrs Blundell of Crosby*

22. THE CHURCH & THE MODERN AGE · *Christopher Hollis*

23. THE PRAYER OF ST THÉRÈSE OF LISIEUX · *Vernon Johnson*

24. THE PROBLEM OF EVIL · *Martin D'Arcy SJ*

25. WHO IS ST JOSEPH? · *Herbert Cardinal Vaughan*